I WONDER WHAT I WOULD SEE...

WRITTEN BY: GEORGETTE GANESH
PHOTOS BY: TIM HOBSON

To order additional copies of this book, contact:
Xlibris
1-888-795-4274
www.Xlibris.com
Orders@Xlibris.com

IN THE OCEAN

&

IN THE JUNGLE

WRITTEN BY: GEORGETTE GANESH

PHOTOS BY: TIM HOBSON

IN THE OCEAN

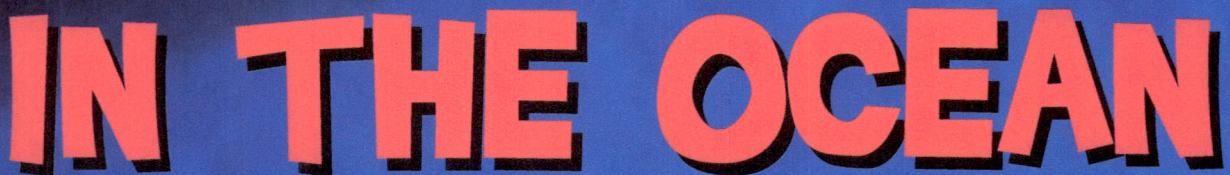

It would be cool

to live in the ocean.

I wonder what

I would see?

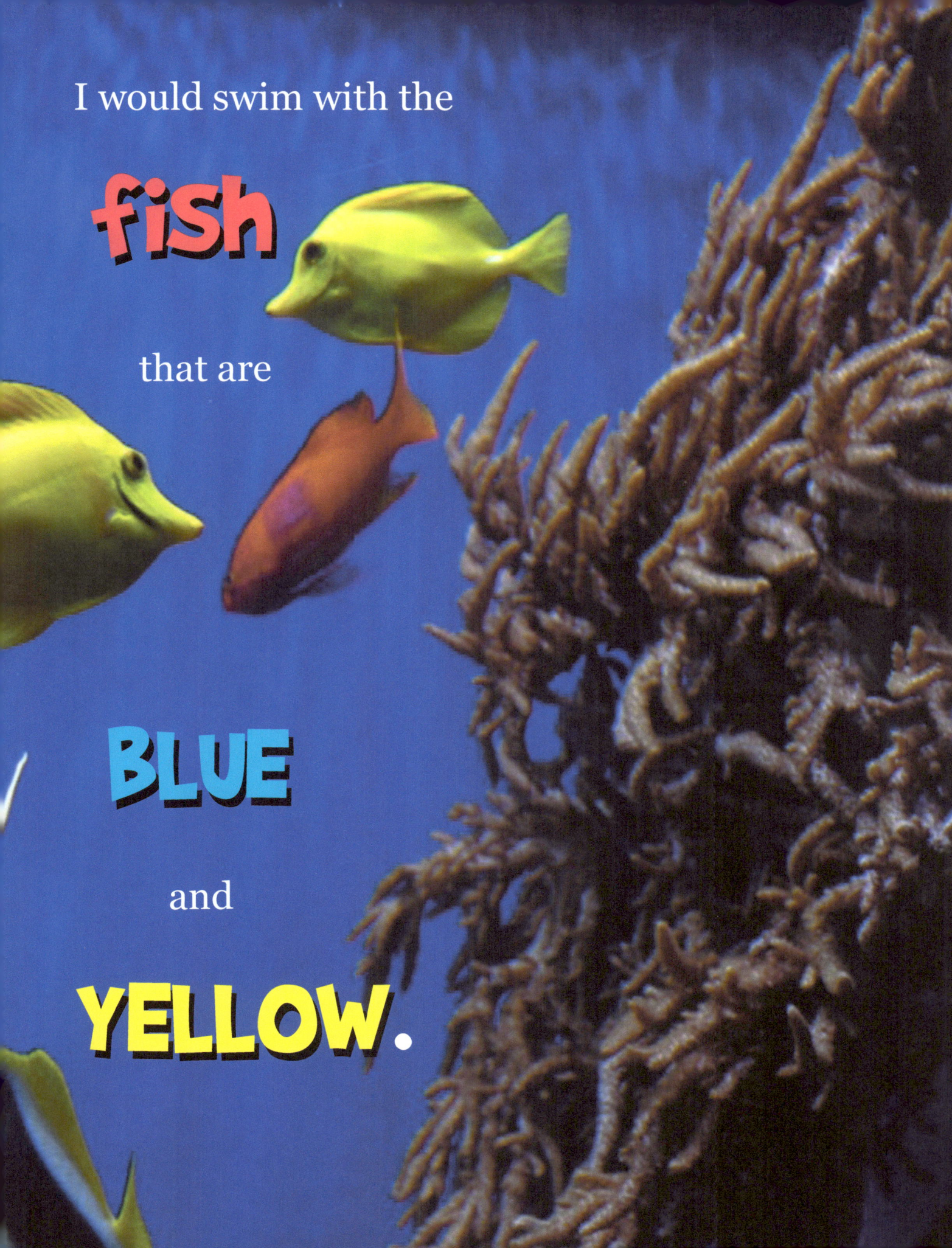

I would swim with the

fish

that are

BLUE

and

YELLOW.

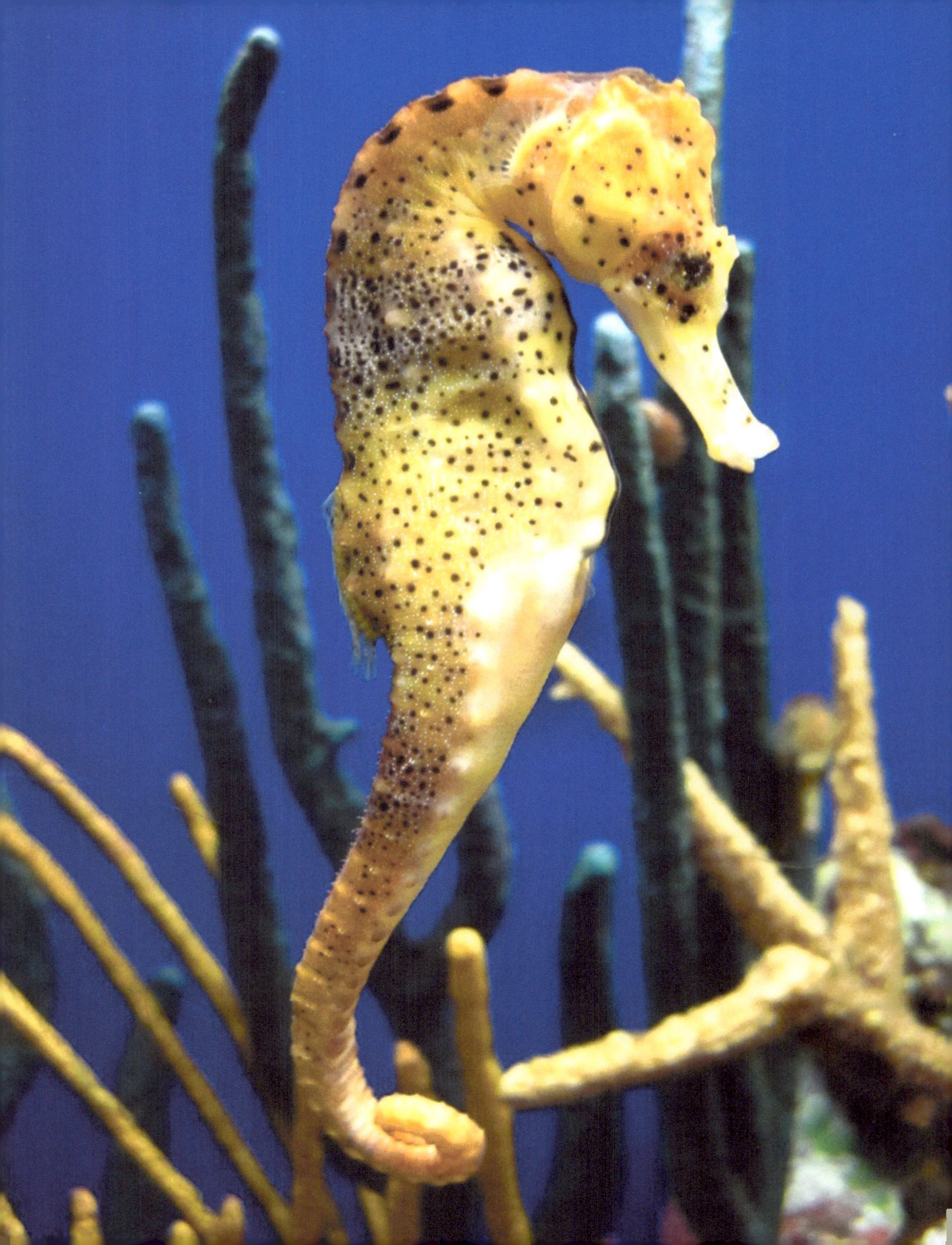

And watch the

seahorses

that are

SLOW

and

MELLOW.

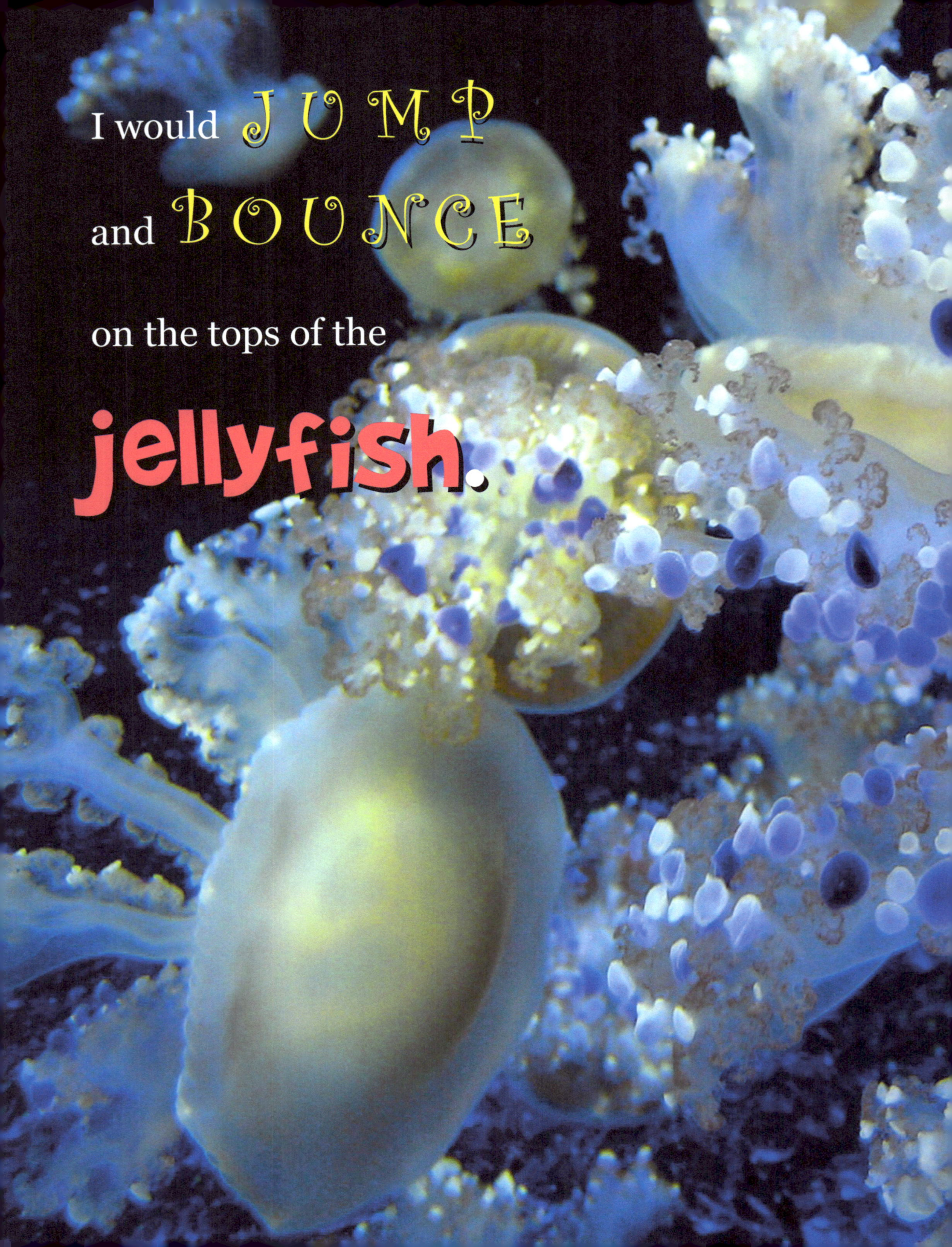

I would JUMP

and BOUNCE

on the tops of the

jellyfish.

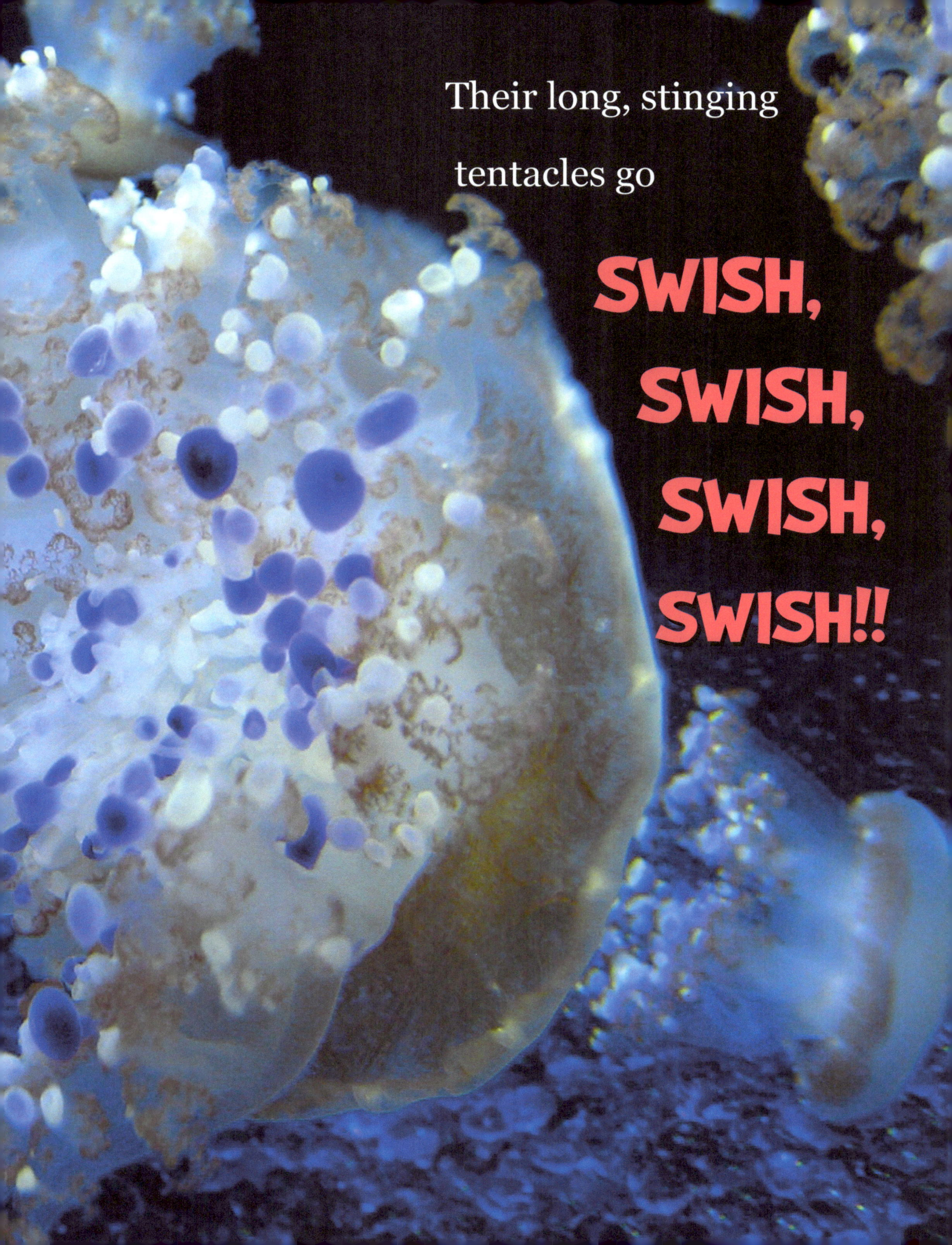

Their long, stinging tentacles go

SWISH, SWISH, SWISH, SWISH!!

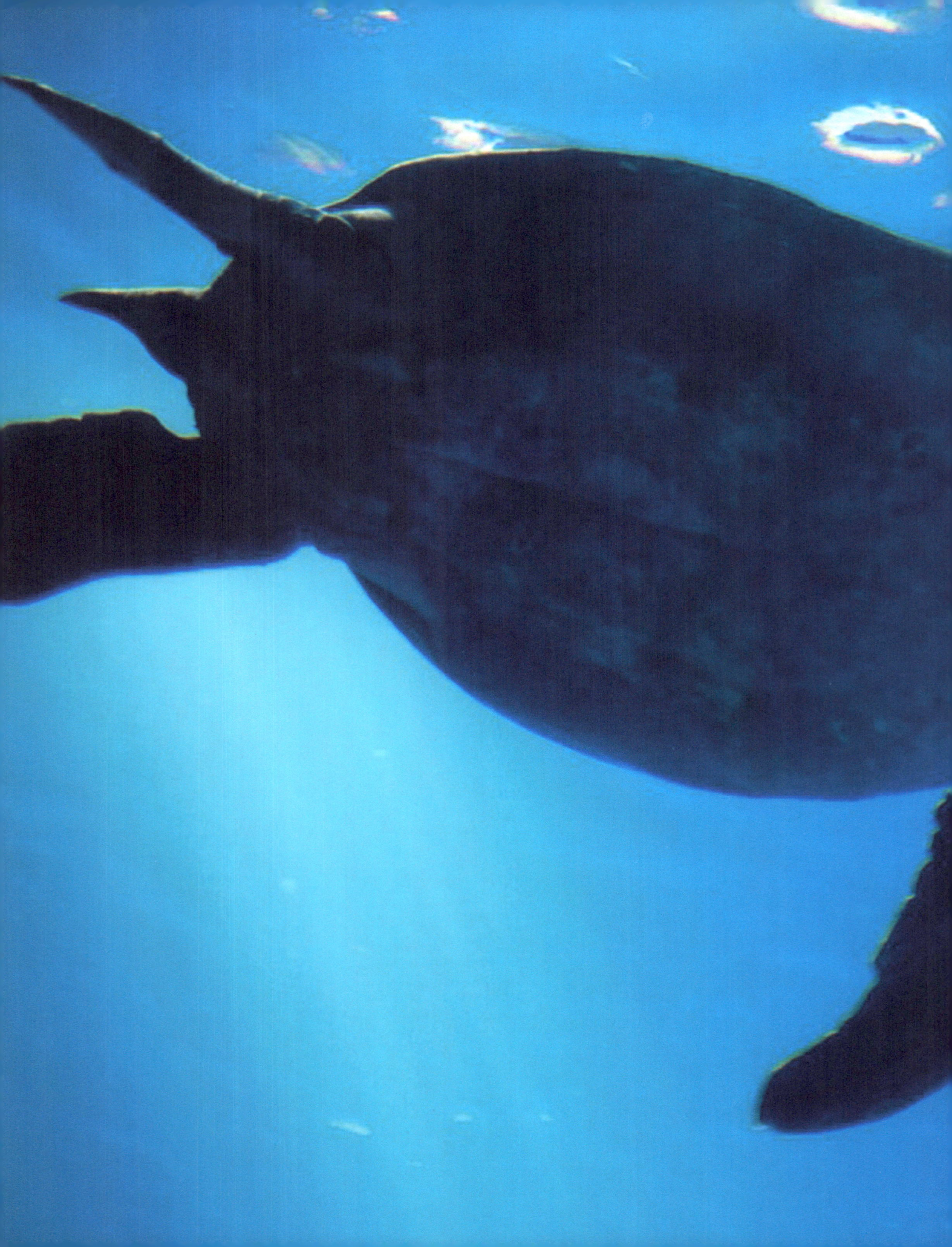

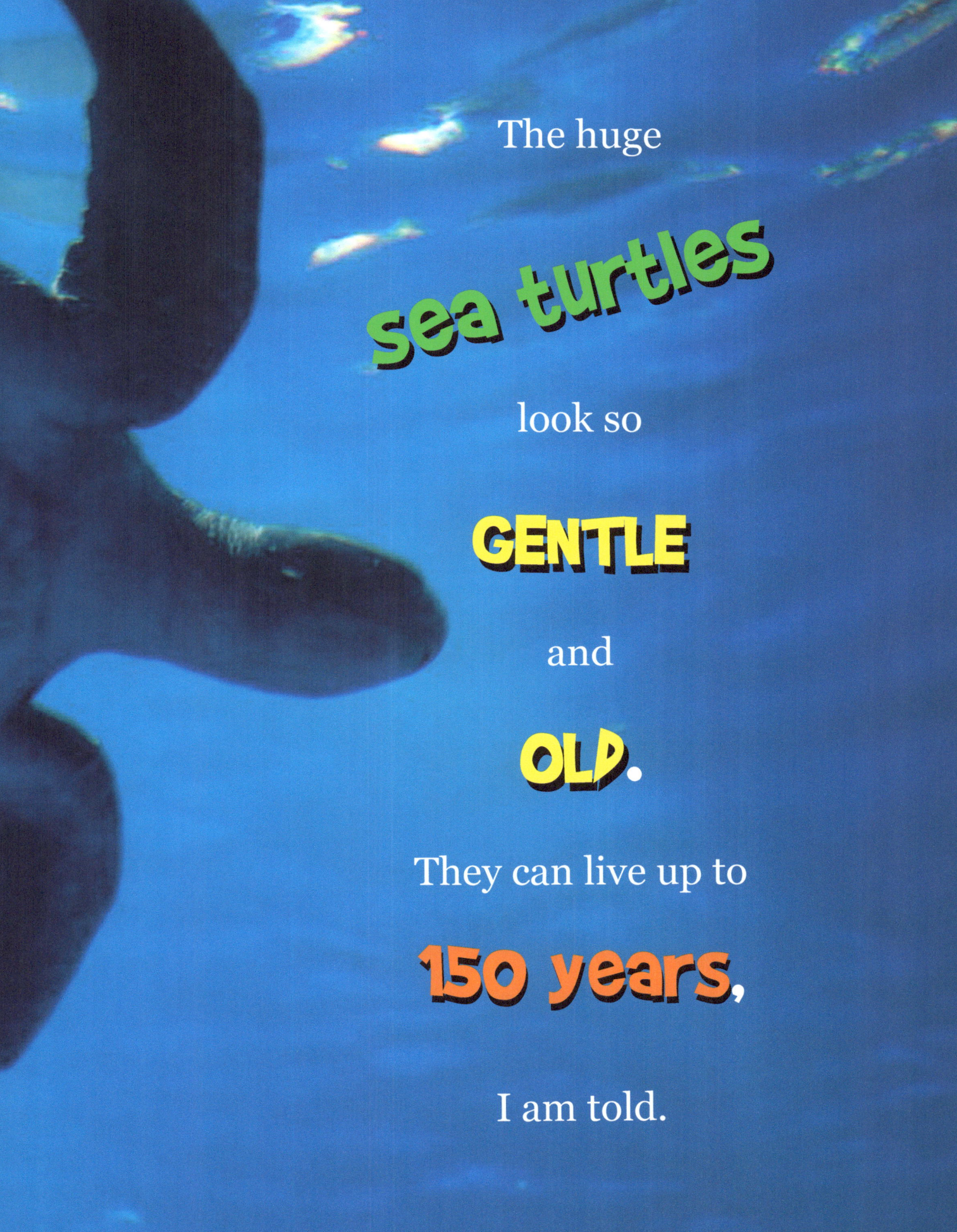

The huge

sea turtles

look so

GENTLE

and

OLD.

They can live up to

150 years,

I am told.

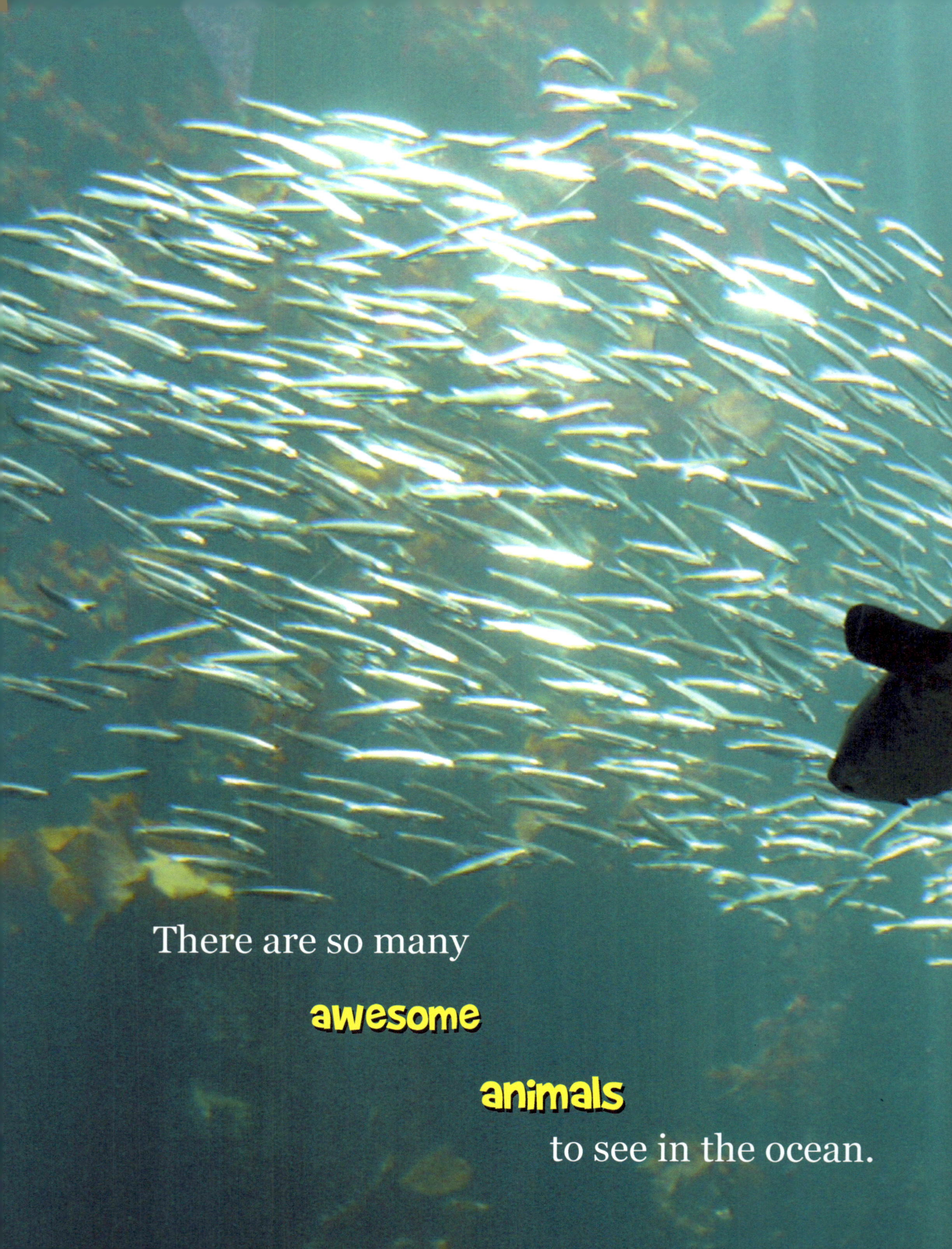

There are so many

awesome

animals

to see in the ocean.

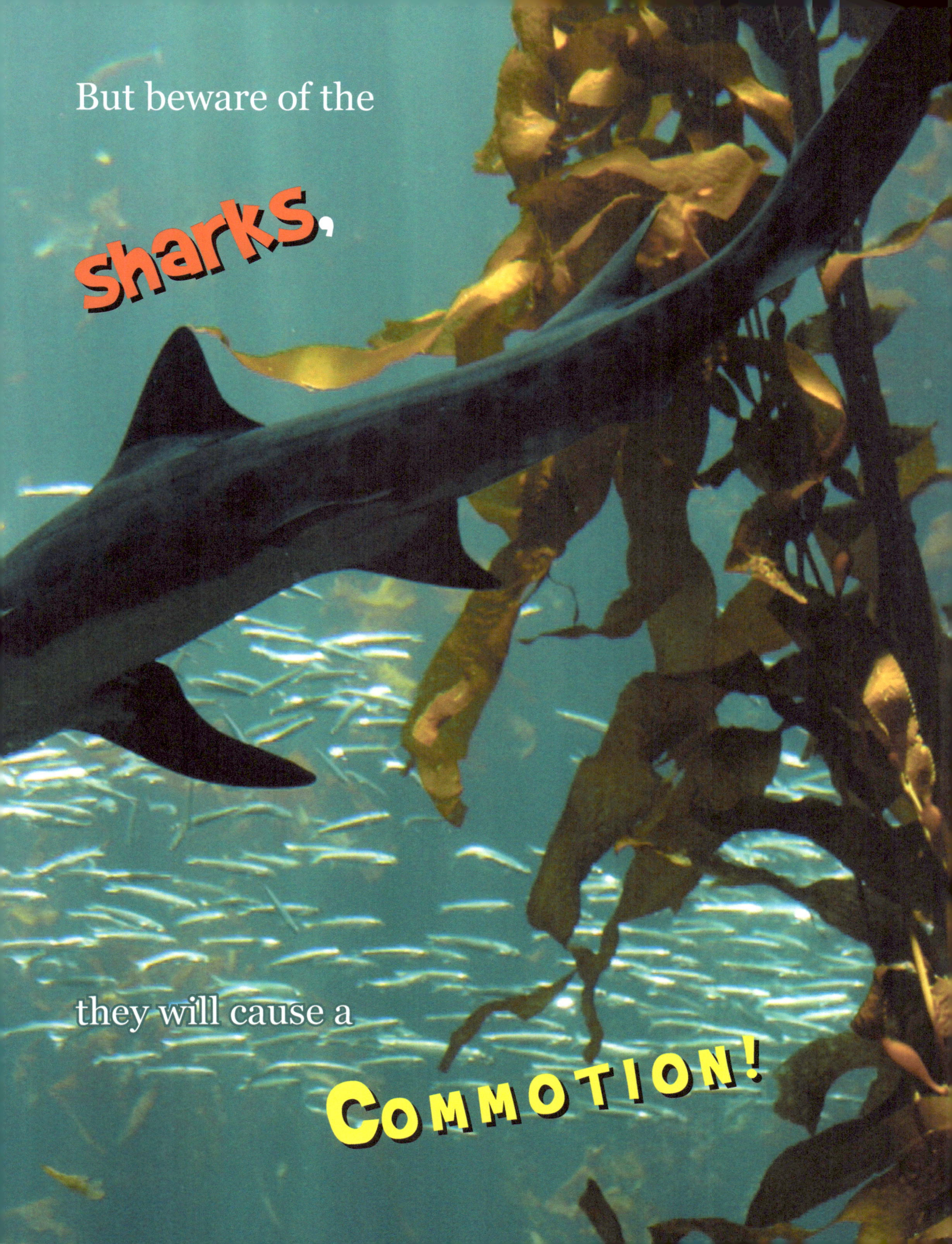

But beware of the

sharks,

they will cause a

COMMOTION!

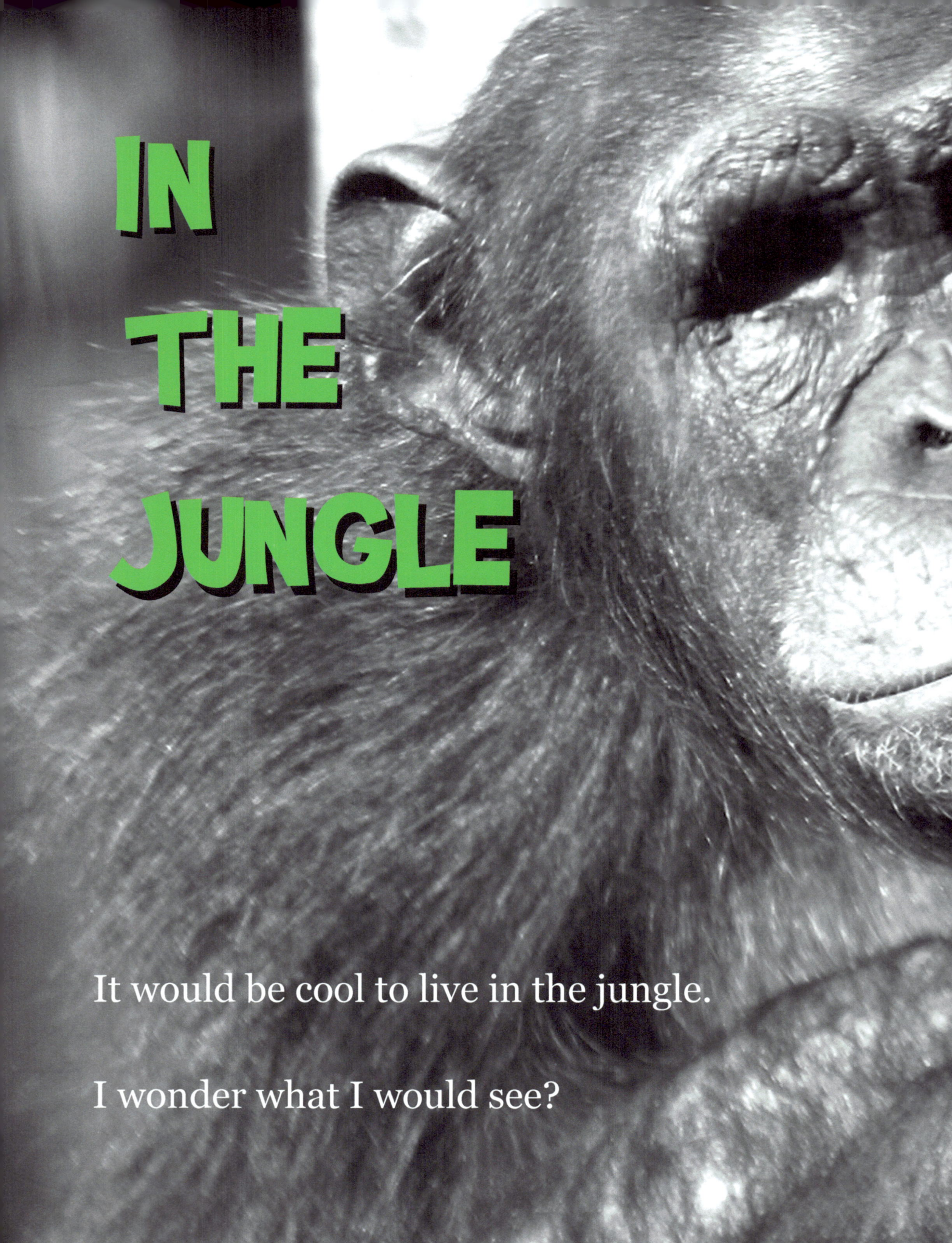

IN THE JUNGLE

It would be cool to live in the jungle.

I wonder what I would see?

The

CHIMPANZEES

would be just like me,

sitting or

playing or

swinging

from a tree.

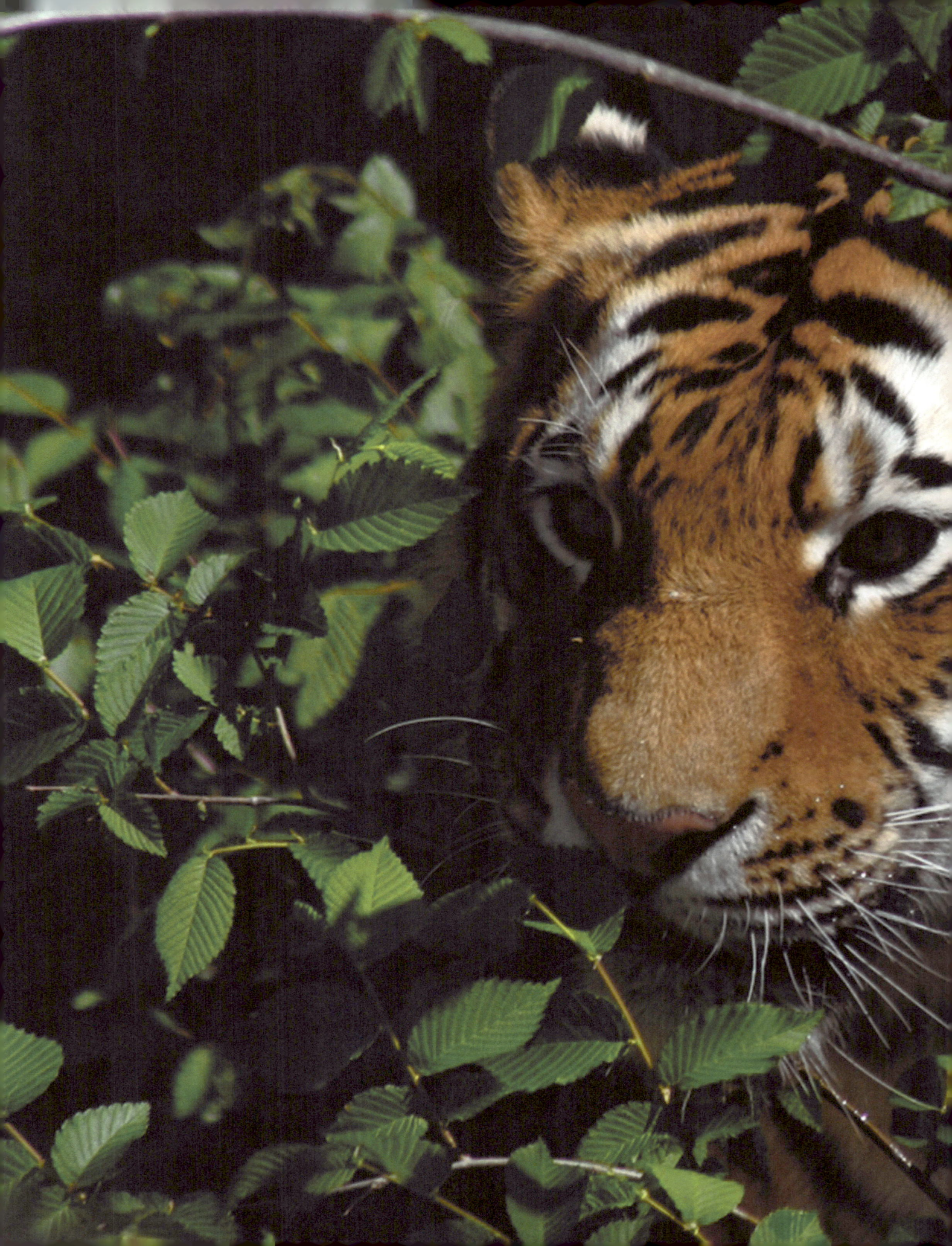

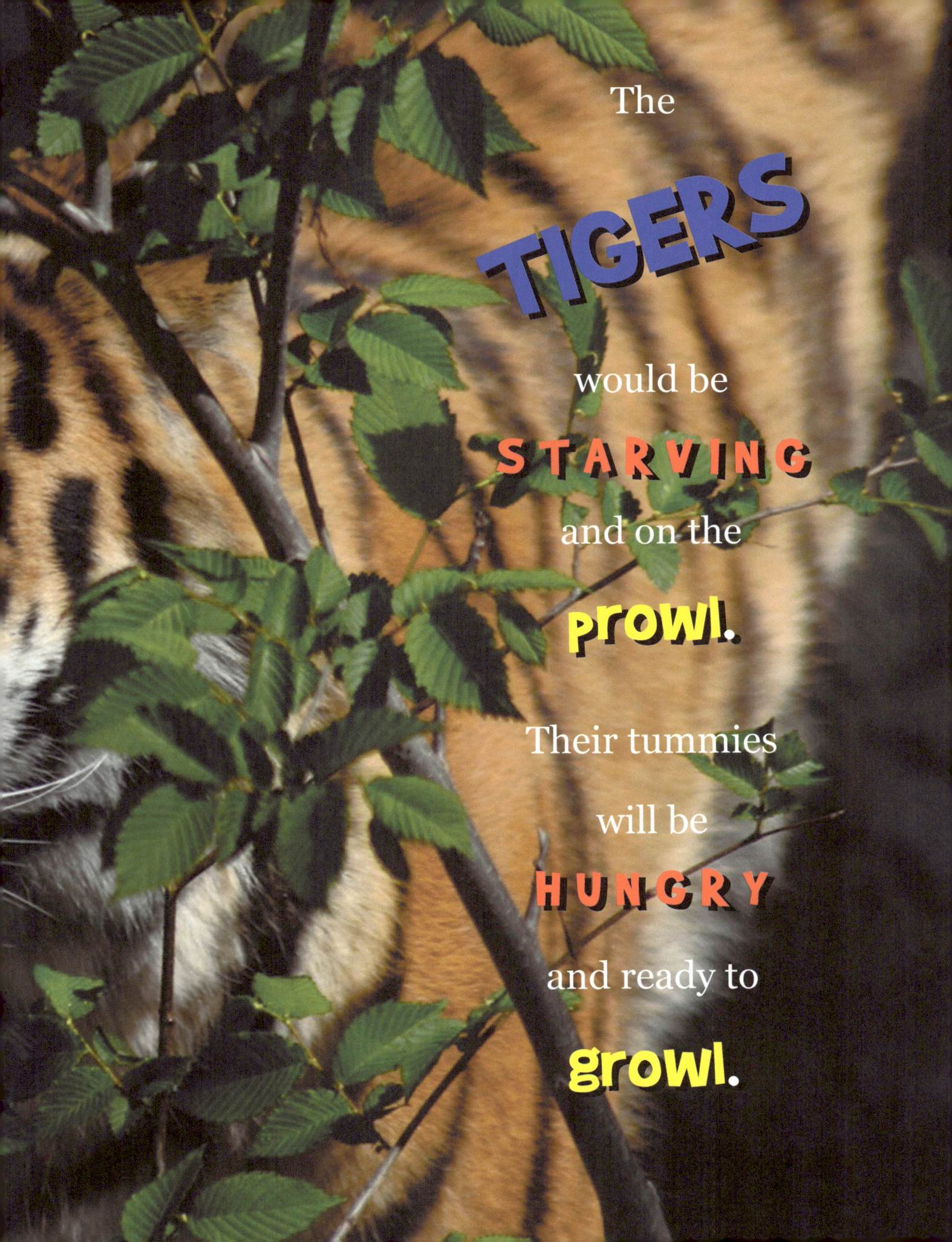

The
TIGERS

would be

STARVING

and on the

prowl.

Their tummies

will be

HUNGRY

and ready to

growl.

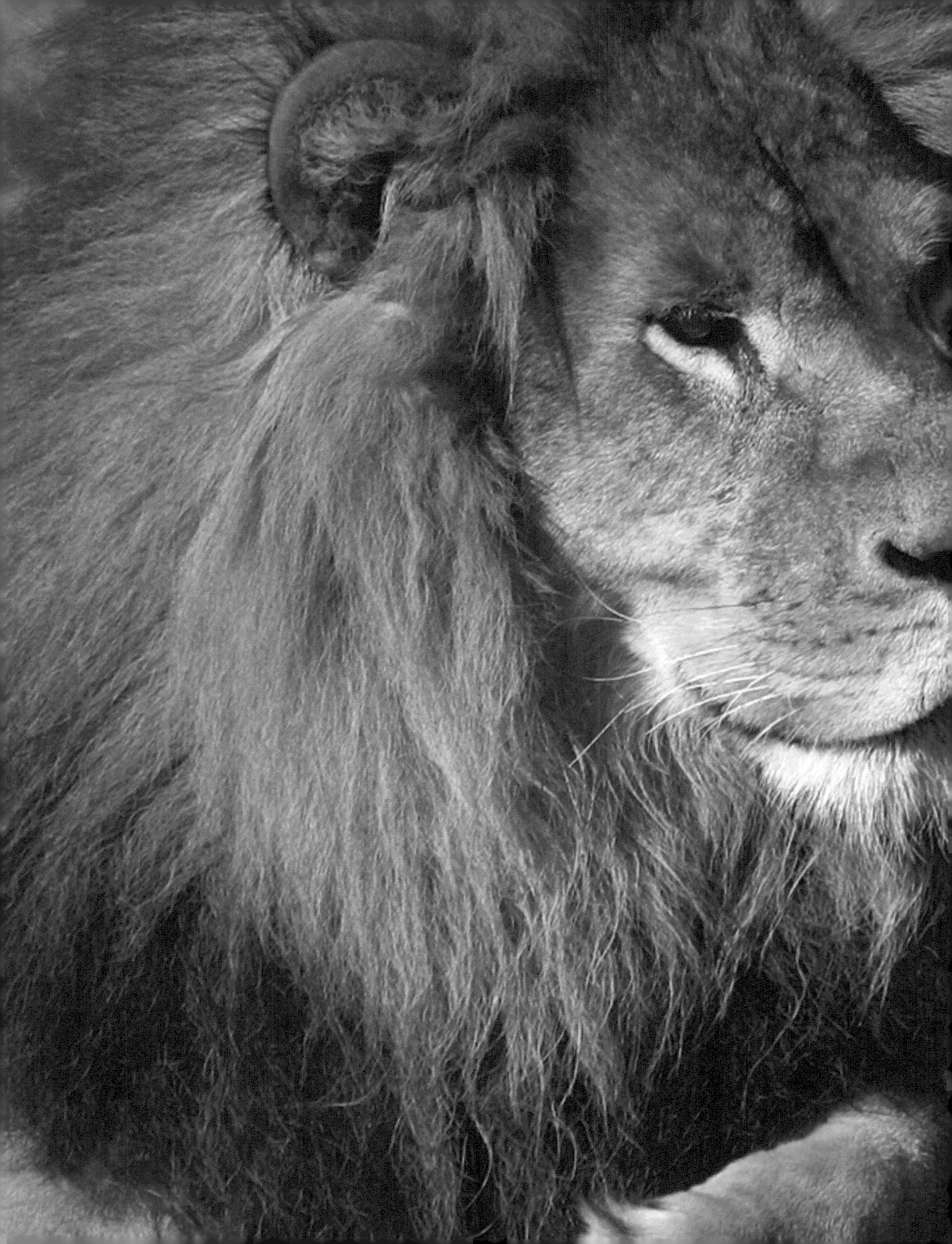

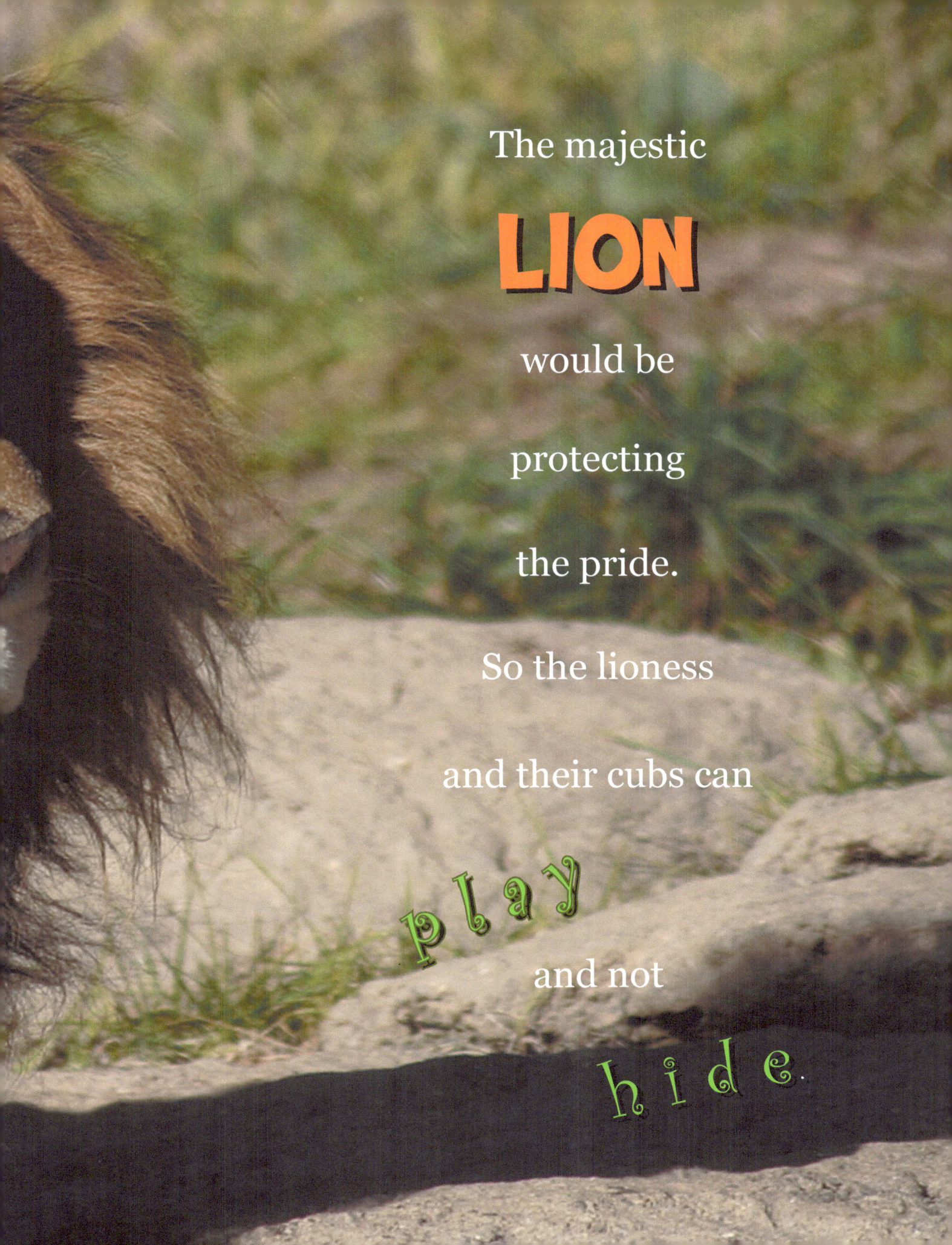

The majestic

LION

would be

protecting

the pride.

So the lioness

and their cubs can

play

and not

hide.

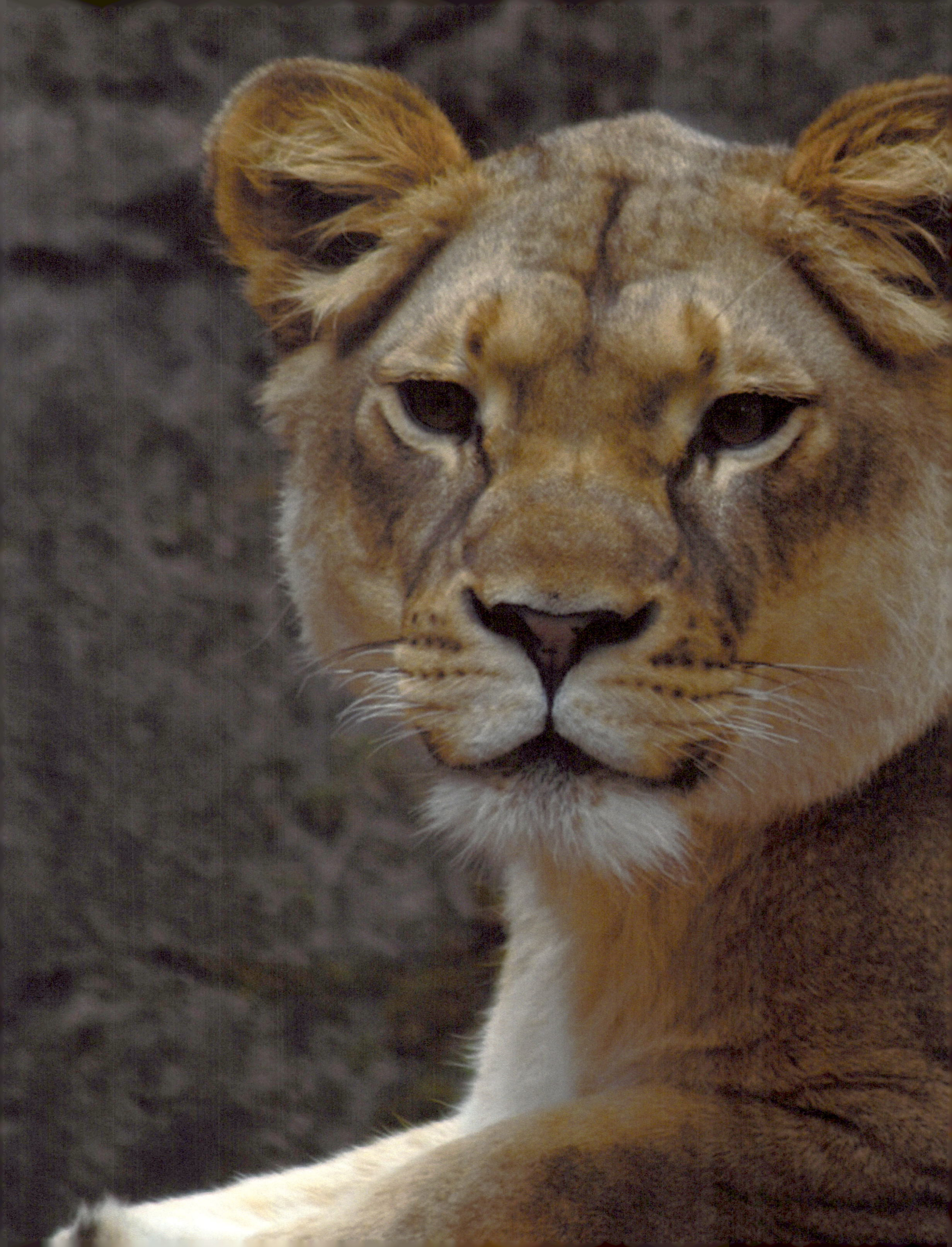

The skillful

LIONESSES

would hunt for the

FOOD.

The lion

would eat first

so he is in

a good

MOOD.

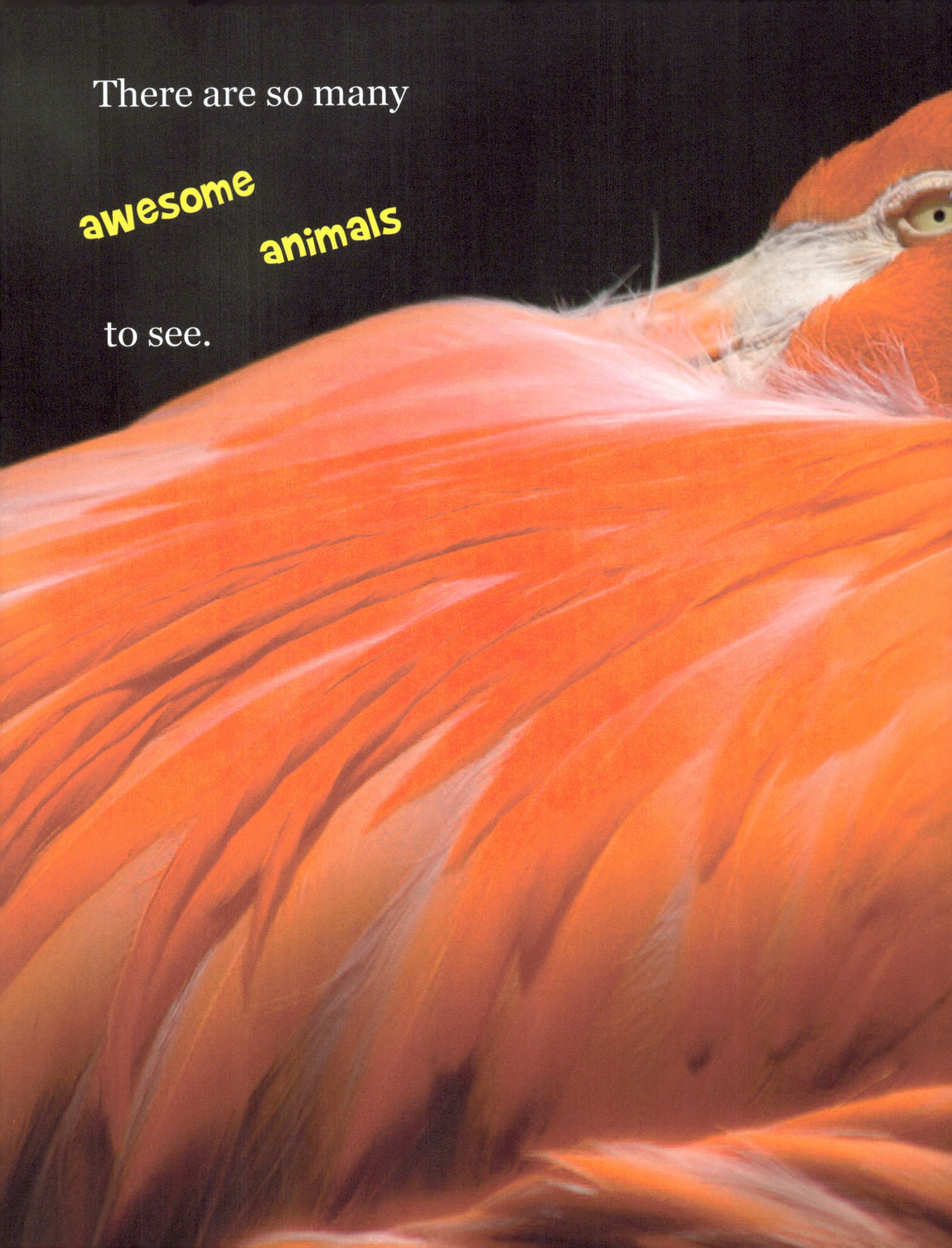

There are so many *awesome* *animals* to see.

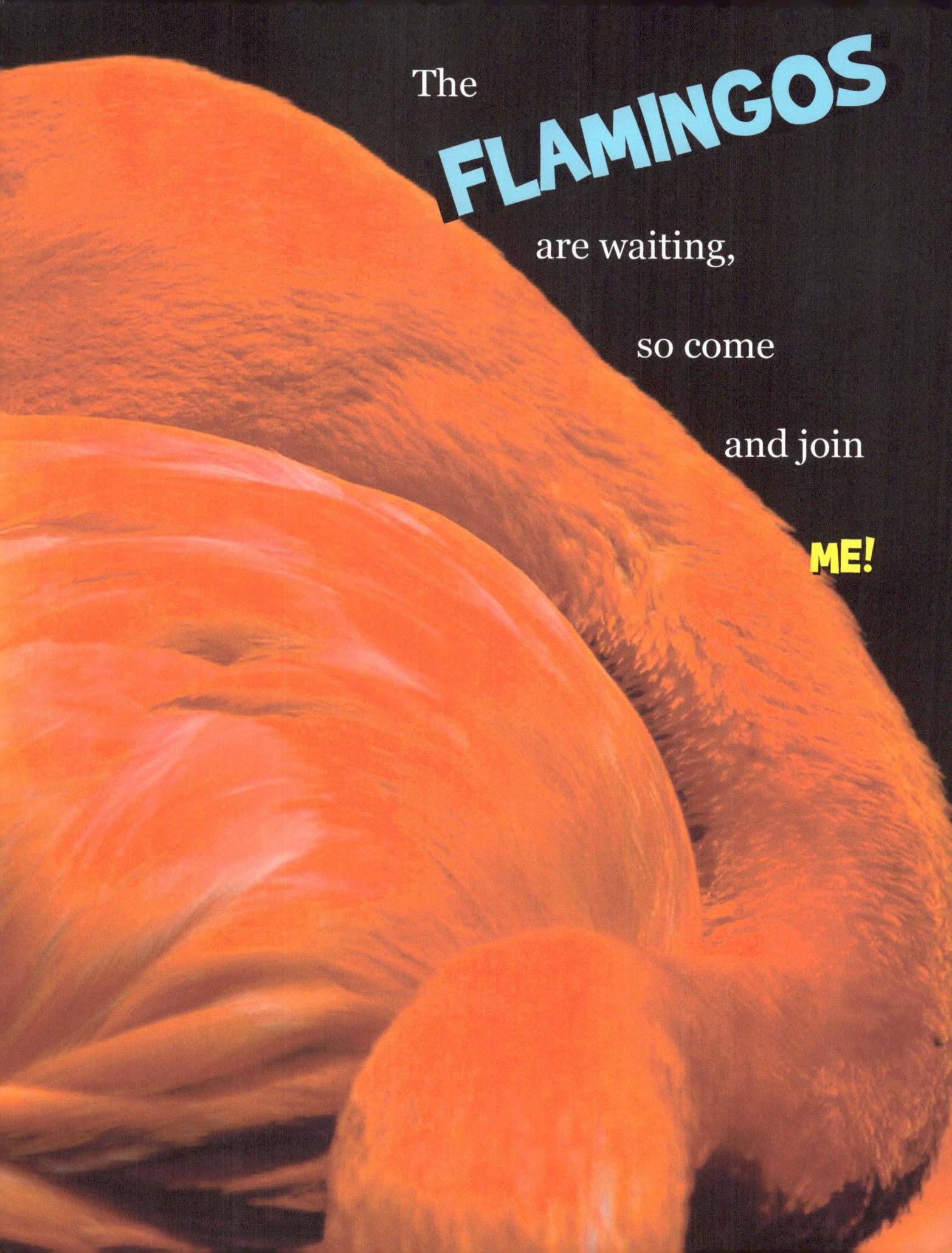

The **FLAMINGOS** are waiting, so come and join ME!